# Animal Tracks
## OF THE ROCKY MOUNTAINS

Jonathan Poppele

*Adventure Quick Guides*

YOUR WAY TO EASILY IDENTIFY ANIMAL TRACKS

# Adventure Quick Guides

Organized by track group for quick and easy identification, this guide has 58 entries covering more than 115 species of four-legged mammals commonly found in the Rocky Mountains.

## HELPFUL NOTES FOR USING THIS QUICK GUIDE:

- Use the Tracking Tips to learn about the basics of tracking and the Track Group Chart to determine which group a track belongs to.

- Individual tracks show a great deal of variation. Use track size, gait (track pattern) and habitat as additional clues when identifying a print.

- The measurements in this guide represent an average range for the species. Individual prints may vary widely from these ranges, especially in soft or loose ground such as snow, sand or mud.

- The most common gait is shown for each species. Some species, such as tree squirrels, show little variation. Other species, such as coyotes, display a wide variety of gaits.

## JONATHAN POPPELE

Jonathan Poppele is an award-winning nature guidebook author and naturalist. He earned a Masters Degree in Conservation Biology studying traditional animal tracking in the mountains of Idaho, is certified in Track & Sign identification by Cyber-Tracker International, and is the founder of the Minnesota Wildlife Tracking Project. You can contact him through the project's website at www.mntracking.org.

10 9 8 7 6 5 4 3

Cover design by Jonathan Norberg
Interior design by Lora Westberg
Illustrations by Julie Martinez and Bruce Wilson

Cover photo: *Bighorn Sheep* by IPK Photography

All images copyrighted. Images by contributing photographers:
**Mary Clay/Dembinsky Photo Associates:** Spotted Skunk **C. Michael Hogan:** Western Harvest Mouse **Dave Kirkeby:** Pocket Gopher **John Kormendy:** Ringtail **Dr. Richard Forbes, owned by Northwest Power & Conservation Council:** Bushy-tailed Woodrat **Stephen Pollard:** Hispid Cotton Rat **Jonathan Poppele:** Mountain Goat **Stan Tekiela:** Masked Shrew, Ord's Kangaroo Rat, Silky Pocket Mouse, Northern Flying Squirrel, Black Mink **US Forest Service:** Western Jumping Mouse
All other images via Shutterstock.

**Animal Tracks of the Rocky Mountains**
Copyright © 2017 by Jonathan Poppele
Published by Adventure Publications
An imprint of AdventureKEEN
All rights reserved
Printed in China
ISBN 978-1-59193-698-5 (pbk.)

### Shrews
FRONT: L ³⁄₁₆"–⁵⁄₁₆"; W ³⁄₁₆"–⁵⁄₁₆"
HIND: L ³⁄₁₆"–⁷⁄₁₆"; W ³⁄₁₆"–⁵⁄₁₆"

Tiny, delicate tracks only
visible under ideal conditions.

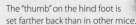

### Harvest Mice
FRONT: L ¼"–³⁄₈"; W ¼"–⁵⁄₁₆"
HIND: L ¼"–½"; W ³⁄₁₆"–⁵⁄₁₆"

The "thumb" on the hind foot is
set farther back than in other mice.

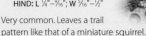

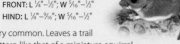

### White-footed Mice
FRONT: L ¼"–½"; W ⁵⁄₁₆"–½"
HIND: L ¼"–⁹⁄₁₆"; W ⁵⁄₁₆"–½"

Very common. Leaves a trail
pattern like that of a miniature squirrel.

### Voles & Lemmings
FRONT: L ¼"–½"; W ¼"–½"
HIND: L ¼"–⁵⁄₈"; W ¼"–½"

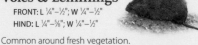

Common around fresh vegetation.
Usually walks, rather than bounds.

## House Mouse

**FRONT:** L ¼"–½"; W ⁵⁄₁₆"–½"
**HIND:** L ¼"–⁹⁄₁₆"; W ⁵⁄₁₆"–½"

Common in and around buildings.
Usually walks rather than bounds.

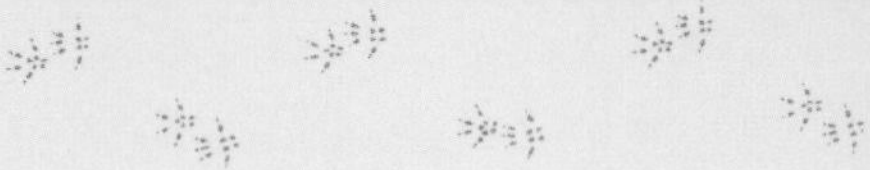

## Jumping Mice

**FRONT:** L ⅜"–⅝"; W ⅜"–⅝"
**HIND:** L ½"–1⅛"; W ⅜"–¾"

Hibernates through the winter.
Has extremely long, slender toes.

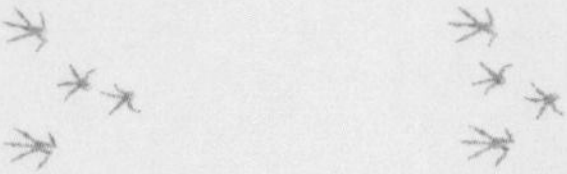

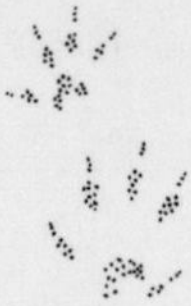

## Pocket Mice

**FRONT:** L ¼"–⅜"; W ¼"–⅜"
**HIND:** L ⅜"–½"; W ¼"–½"

Only four toes show clearly on the
hind foot. Pads are often indistinct.

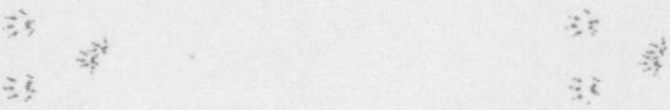

## Ord's Kangaroo Rat

**FRONT:** L ¼"–½"; W ¼"–⅜"
**HIND:** L ⅜"–1¼"; W ⅜"–¾"

Usually leaves only hind prints.
Hind tracks show only four toes.

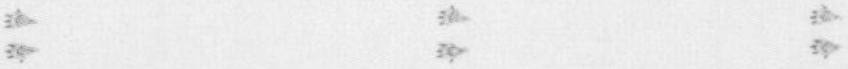

## Hispid Cotton Rat
**FRONT:** L ⅜"–½"; W ⅜"–½" 
**HIND:** L ⁷⁄₁₆"–¹¹⁄₁₆"; W ⁷⁄₁₆"–⁹⁄₁₆"

Found only in SE CO. Tracks are larger than a mouse's but smaller than a Norway rat's.

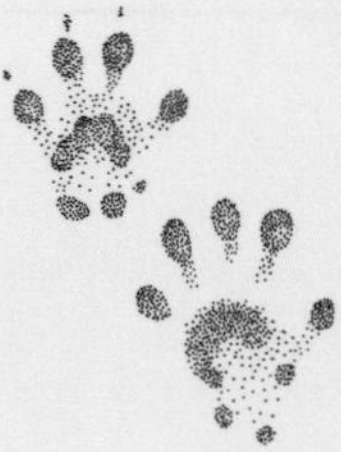

## Woodrats
**FRONT:** L ⅜"–⅞"; W ⅜"–¾"
**HIND:** L ½"–1¼"; W ½"–⅞"

More bulbous toe pads than in other small rodents.

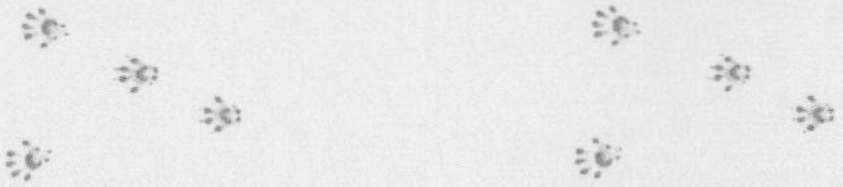

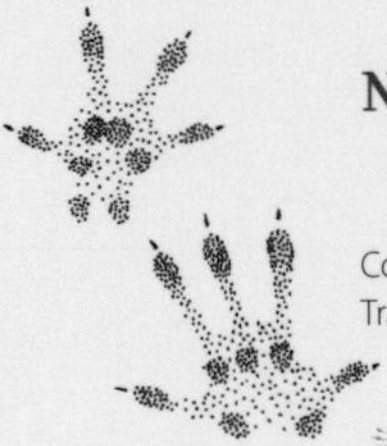

## Norway Rat
**FRONT:** L ½"–¾"; W ½"–¾"
**HIND:** L ⅝"–1¼"; W ⅝"–1"

Common around buildings. Tracks are mouse-like but much larger.

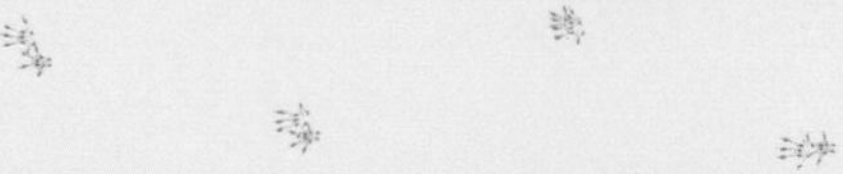

## Pocket Gophers
**FRONT:** L ¾"–1¼"; W ⅜"–⅞" 
**HIND:** L ⅞"–1⅛"; W ⅜"–⅞"

Digging signs are often conspicuous, but tracks are uncommon.

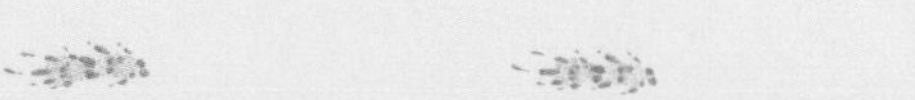

## Chipmunks

FRONT: L ½"–⅞"; W ⅜"–¾"
HIND: L ½"–1"; W ½"–⅞"

Tracks and trails similar to those of tree squirrels, but smaller.

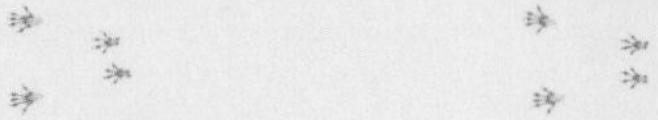

## Northern Flying Squirrel

FRONT: L ½"–1"; W ½"–¾"
HIND: L 1¼"–1¾"; W ⅝"–⅞"

Front feet usually land wide apart, creating a "boxy" track pattern.

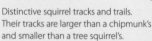

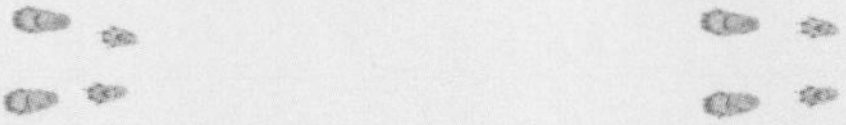

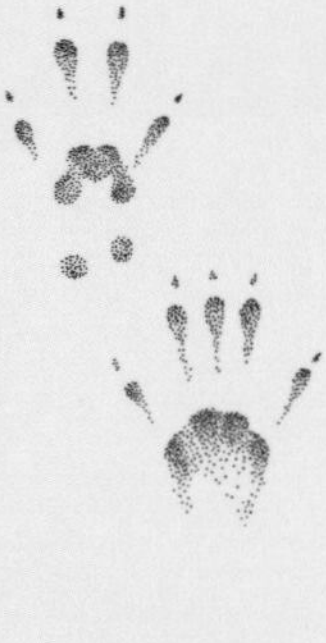

## Red Squirrel

FRONT: L ⅞"–1¼"; W ½"–1"
HIND: L 1"–2"; W ¾"–1¼"

Distinctive squirrel tracks and trails. Their tracks are larger than a chipmunk's and smaller than a tree squirrel's.

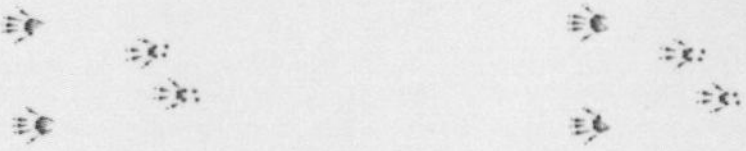

## Tree Squirrels

FRONT: L 1"–1¾"; W ½"–1½"
HIND: L 1"–2¾"; W ⅞"–1¾"

Distinctive squirrel trail patterns. Trails usually begin and end at trees.

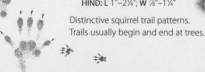

## Ground Squirrels

**FRONT: L** ¾"–1⅜"; **W** ⅜"–1"
**HIND: L** ¾"–1½"; **W** ⅝"–1⅜"

Front tracks have prominent claws.
Hibernates for much of the year.

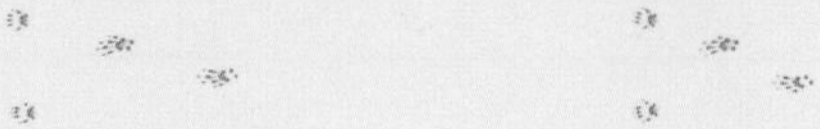

## Prairie Dog

**FRONT: L** 1"–1½"; **W** ⅞"–1⅜"
**HIND: L** 1"–2"; **W** ⅞"–1⅜"

Lives in large, unmistakable
communal burrows.

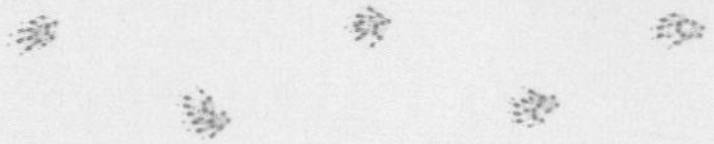

## Marmot

**FRONT: L** 1½"–2¾"; **W** 1¼"–2"
**HIND: L** 1⅜"–3"; **W** 1¼"–2"

Large, squirrel-like tracks.
Typically walks rather than bounds.

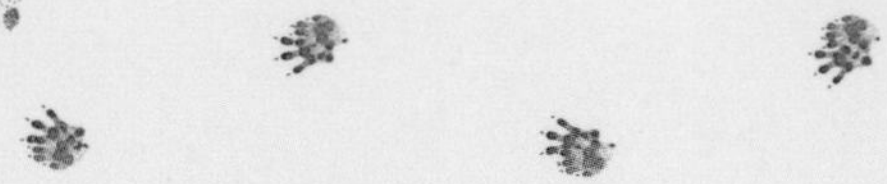

### Muskrat
**FRONT:** L 1"–1½"; W 1"–1½"
**HIND:** L 1½"–2½"; W 1⅜"–2¼"

Usually found near water. Long, stout hind toes are fringed with stiff hairs.

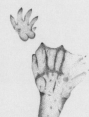

### North American Porcupine
**FRONT:** L 2¼"–3¼"; W 1½"–1⅞"
**HIND:** L 2¾"–4"; W 1¼"–2"

Oval tracks with a unique "pebbly" texture. Toes rarely show.

### American Beaver
**FRONT:** L 2"–3½"; W 1½"–3"
**HIND:** L 4½"–7"; W 3"–5"

Clear hind prints are unmistakable. Trails usually lead to or from water.

### American Pika
**FRONT:** L ⅝"–¾"; W ⅜"–¾"
**HIND:** L ⅝"–1"; W ⅝"–⅞"

Lives in rocky terrain at high elevations. Clear prints are rare.

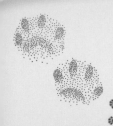

## Cottontail Rabbits

**FRONT:** L ⅞"–1¾"; W ⅝"–1¼"
**HIND:** L 1¼"–3¼"; W ¾"–1⅝"

Very common. Egg-shaped tracks. Distinctive rabbit trail pattern.

## Snowshoe Hare

**FRONT:** L 1¾"–3"; W 1¼"–2¼"
**HIND:** L 3"–5"; W 1½"–4½"

Hind tracks can be much larger than front. Distinctive rabbit trail pattern.

## Black-tailed Jackrabbit

**FRONT:** L 1⅝"–2½"; W 1¼"–1¾"
**HIND:** L 2"–5"; W 1¼"–2½"

Hind heel rarely shows. Has a broader range of gaits than most other rabbits.

## White-tailed Jackrabbit

**FRONT:** L 2⅛"–3¾"; W 1½"–2½"
**HIND:** L 3"–6½"; W 1½"–3"

Hind heel rarely shows. Hind tracks are typically offset from each other.

## Striped Skunk

**FRONT:** L ⅞"–1¾"; W ⅞"–1¼"
**HIND:** L 1"–1¾"; W ⅞"–1¼"

Prominent claws. Toes never splay. Trails resemble those of a miniature bear.

## Western Spotted Skunk

**FRONT:** L 1"–1⅜"; W ¾"–1"
**HIND:** L ¾"–1¼"; W ⅝"–1⅛"

Tracks have clean, compact look. Prominent claws. Irregular gaits.

## Weasels

**FRONT:** L ⁵⁄₁₆"–½"; W ⁵⁄₁₆"–½"
**HIND:** L ⁵⁄₁₆"–½"; W ⁵⁄₁₆"–½"

Small tracks, typically in a 2x2 lope with highly variable strides.

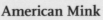

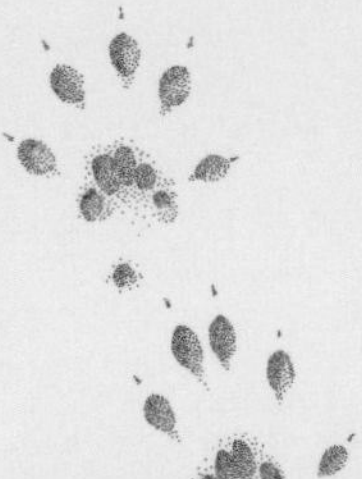

## American Mink

**FRONT:** L 1"–1¾"; W ¾"–1⅝"
**HIND:** L ¾"–1½"; W ⅞"–1⅝"

Crisper tracks than in other small weasels. Usually found close to water.

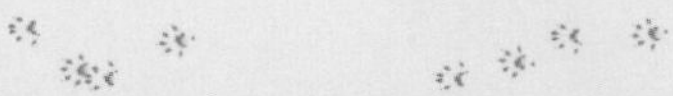

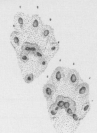

## American Marten

**FRONT: L** 1½"–2¾"; **W** 1⅜"–2½"
**HIND: L** 1½"–2⅝"; **W** 1⅜"–2½"

Thick fur blurs palm and toe pads.
Trails often end at the base of a tree.

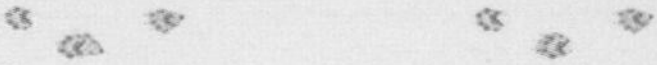

## American Badger

**FRONT: L** 1⅞"–2⅝"; **W** 1½"–2¾"
**HIND: L** 1½"–2½"; **W** 1¼"–2¼"

Walks with toes turned
in. Long claws leave
prominent marks.

## River Otter

**FRONT: L** 2"–3"; **W** 1⅞"–3"
**HIND: L** 2¼"–3¾"; **W** 2⅛"–3½"

Usually found near water.
Trails often include slides.
May show tail drag.

## Wolverine

**FRONT: L** 3½"–6"; **W** 3½"–4½"
**HIND: L** 3⅛"–6"; **W** 3"–5¼"

Thick fur can obscure track
detail. Inner toe may not register, leaving
a track similar to that of a large canine or feline.

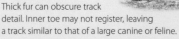

## Ringtail

**FRONT:** L 1"–1½"; W 1"–1⅜"
**HIND:** L 1"–1½"; W ⅞"–1¼"

Tracks resemble those of house cats but have a larger palm pad. Claws rarely register.

## Northern Raccoon

**FRONT:** L 1¾"–2¾"; W 1½"–2¾"
**HIND:** L 2"–2¾"; W 1½"–2¾"

Distinctive 2x2 walking gait. Tracks often resemble human handprints.

## Black Bear

**FRONT:** L 3½"–6"; W 3½"–5½"
**HIND:** L 5"–8"; W 3½"–5¾"

Huge. Five toes and robust palm pad. Clear prints can only be mistaken for brown bear tracks.

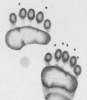

## Brown Bear

**FRONT:** L 4"–10½"; W 4⅛"–7⅛"
**HIND:** L 4¼"–11"; W 4"–7"

Huge. Generally larger than black bear tracks with front toes forming a straighter line and showing longer claws.

## Kit Fox & Swift Fox

**FRONT:** L 1"–1½"; W 1"–1½"
**HIND:** L 1"–1½"; W ⅞"–1¼"

Smallest wild canine track in the Rockies. Hind palm may not register.

## Gray Fox

**FRONT:** L 1¼"–1¾"; W 1¼"–1¾"
**HIND:** L 1⅛"–1¾"; W 1"–1⅝"

Claws may not show. Trails may begin or end at the base of a tree.

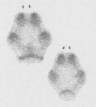

## Red Fox

**FRONT:** L 1¾"–2½"; W 1½"–2⅛"
**HIND:** L 1½"–2½"; W 1¼"–1⅞"

Heavy fur often makes pads less distinct than those of other canines.

## Coyote

**FRONT:** L 2"–3"; W 1½"–2¾"
**HIND:** L 2"–3"; W 1⅜"–2¼"

Tracks usually narrower than in other canines. Hind palm may not register.

## Gray Wolf

**FRONT:** L 3¼"–4½"; W 2¾"–4"
**HIND:** L 3"–4¼"; W 2½"–3¼"

Strong toes may pull soil into a dome between the pads. Very large tracks.

### House Cat

FRONT: L 1"–1⅝"; W 1"–1¾"
HIND: L 1⅛"–1⅝"; W ⅞"–1⅝"

Tracks are round with a large palm pad. Claws rarely show.

### Bobcat

FRONT: L 1½"–2½"; W 1½"–2½"
HIND: L 1½"–2½"; W 1¼"–2¼"

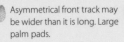

Asymmetrical front track may be wider than it is long. Large palm pads.

### Canada Lynx

FRONT: L 2¾"–4"; W 2⅝"–4½"
HIND: L 2¾"–4"; W 2½"–4¼"

Heavily furred feet often make pads look small and indistinct.

### Cougar

FRONT: L 2¾"–4"; W 2¾"–4½"
HIND: L 2¾"–4"; W 2½"–4¼"

Large palm pad. The largest track in our region that doesn't show claws.

## Pronghorn

**FRONT:** L 2⅛"–3¼"; W 1½"–2⅜"
**HIND:** L 2⅛"–3"; W 1½"–2⅛"

Narrow heart-shaped track. Center of the track is often slightly raised.

## Mule Deer

**FRONT:** L 2"–3½"; W 1¾"–2¾"
**HIND:** L 1⅞"–3¼"; W 1½"–2½"

Extremely abundant. Distinctive and familiar heart-shaped track.

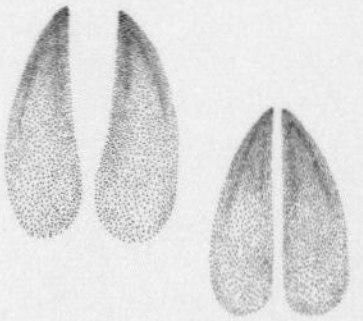

## White-tailed Deer

**FRONT:** L 2"–3½"; W 1⅝"–2¾"
**HIND:** L 1⅞"–3¼"; W 1½"–2½"

Nearly identical to Mule Deer tracks. Use habitat and range to help distinguish tracks.

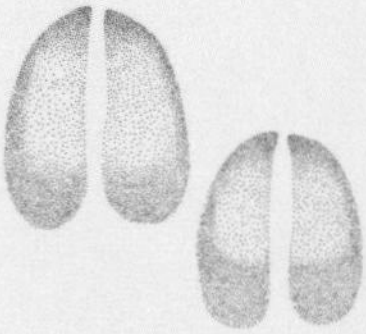

## Elk

**FRONT:** L 3¼"–4¾"; W 2¾"–4¼"
**HIND:** L 2⅞"–4¼"; W 2⅜"–3¾"

Large tracks are rounder than those of other members of the deer family.

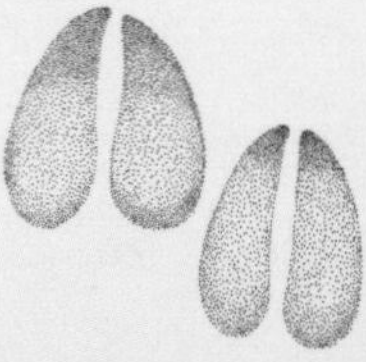

## Moose

**FRONT:** L 4½"–7"; W 3¾"–5¾"
**HIND:** L 4¼"–6½"; W 3½"–5"

Enormous heart-shaped tracks are unmistakable.

## Mountain Goat

**FRONT:** L 2¼"–3¼"; W 2¼"–3¼"
**HIND:** L 2¼"–3"; W 2"–3¾"

Exceptional climbers at home in very steep terrain. Tracks are rounder than those of deer or bighorn sheep.

## Bighorn Sheep

**FRONT:** L 2¼"–3⅜"; W 2"–2¾"
**HIND:** L 2¼"–3⅜"; W 1¾"–2½"

Found on or near steep, rocky slopes. Tracks are rounder than deer, but less round than mountain goat.

## Domestic Cow

**FRONT:** L 2½"–4¾"; W 2¼"–5¾"
**HIND:** L 2½"–4¾"; W 2¼"–4¾"

Large, round tracks. Typically smaller than bison but not always distinguishable.

## Bison

**FRONT:** L 4½"–6½"; W 4½"–6½"
**HIND:** L 4"–6"; W 4"–6"

Enormous round hoof prints; can only be mistaken for tracks of domestic cattle.

## Horse

**FRONT:** L 4¾"–5½"; W 4¼"–5¼"
**HIND:** L 4½"–5¼"; W 4"–4¾"

Large, round, single-toed tracks are unmistakable.

# Individual Track Identification

When looking at individual prints, identify both the front and hind tracks of the animal, if possible. Once you do, these four steps can help you identify the track:

1. Study the overall shape of the track
2. Count the number of toes
3. Look for claws
4. Measure the size of the track

## STEP 1. STUDY THE OVERALL SHAPE OF THE TRACK

Is the track circular, oval or lopsided? Is it wider at the front or wider at the back? Are the toes symmetrically or asymmetrically arranged?

## STEP 2. COUNT THE NUMBER OF TOES

Be careful—there are a lot of things that can confound this seemingly simple task. One or more toes may not register clearly, or toes may be set far off to the side. Stray marks on the ground may look like toes. Try to find a couple of prints from the same foot to verify your count.

## STEP 3. LOOK FOR CLAWS

Some animals, like dogs and skunks, nearly always show claw marks. Others rarely do. While not foolproof, presence or absence of claws is a useful clue for identification.

## STEP 4. MEASURE THE SIZE OF THE TRACK

Measure the track's length and width. While animal foot sizes can vary tremendously within a species, track size will help you narrow down the possibilities.

## HOW TO MEASURE TRACKS

Measure tracks along their longest and widest points. Measure length from the rear edge of the rearmost palm or heel pad to the front edge of the foremost toe pad. The measurements in this guide do not include claws unless they are indistinguishable from the toes or the toes themselves are not visible. Measure width across the widest part of the foot, including all of the toes. Note: Getting accurate measurements can be tricky. Momentum can distort the length of the track, and soft ground, sand and snow can alter track size, and uneven ground can skew shape. Look for clear tracks relatively free from distortion. If you can, measure several tracks to get an average.

# Gaits

Gaits describe the body mechanics of an animal's movement, including the order of its footfalls and how it coordinates its limbs. Each gait leaves a distinctive pattern of tracks. Most mammals in the Rocky Mountains walk on all fours. Four-legged movement is more complicated than two-legged movement and requires some special terminology. Four-legged gaits can be broadly divided into two categories: whole-body gaits and stepping gaits.

## WHOLE-BODY GAITS

In whole-body gaits, the body flexes and extends, and movement is created by the torso and legs working together. These gaits have a syncopated rhythm and produce distinctive groups of four tracks. Whole-body gaits fall into two categories: those where each foot lands independently, called lopes and gallops, and those where the hind feet land together, called hops and bounds.

**Loping and Galloping:** In both lopes and gallops, each foot moves independently as the animal flexes and extends its body. In a lope, at least one hind foot lands behind one of the front feet. In gallops, both hind feet land in front of the front feet. Lopes can be easy, gentle gaits, while gallops are usually all-out sprints. Lopes are the most common gaits for members of the weasel family.

Skunk lope

Wolf gallop

**Hopping and Bounding:** Hops and bounds are distinguished in the same way as lopes and gallops. A gait is a hop when the hind tracks are behind one front track and a bound when they are in front of the front tracks. When bounding, an animal's hind feet straddle its front feet, causing the hind tracks to register wider than in the front. Tree-climbing animals usually bound with their front feet side-by-side, while non-climbers usually place one front foot ahead of the other. Bounding is the most common gait for most small rodents and most members of the rabbit family.

Squirrel bound

Cottontail bound

## STEPPING GAITS

In stepping gaits, an animal keeps its body level and uses only its legs for locomotion. The legs move with an even rhythm and produce a line of evenly spaced pairs of tracks. Stepping gaits can be divided into walks and trots.

**Walking:** When walking, an animal moves each leg independently and always has at least one foot on the ground. Animals can place their hind feet on the ground either behind their front track (understep), on top of it (direct register) or in front of it (overstep). Raccoons use an extreme overstep, placing their hind foot next to the front track on the opposite side of the body. Walking is the most common gait for bears, raccoons, some large rodents and members of the cat and deer families.

Deer walk

Raccoon walk

**Trotting:** When an animal trots, the two legs diagonally opposite each other move at the same time, and there is a split second when the animal has all four feet off the ground. Like walks, trots can be understep, direct register, or overstep. Overstep trots generally require the animal to turn its body slightly, allowing the hind feet to pass to the side of the front feet. Trots are the most common gaits for members of the dog family, as well as some voles and shrews.

Coyote trot

Fox trot

# Photographing Tracks

- **Shoot in the Shade:** Dappled sun is difficult to expose properly; shadows can distort the shape of the track.

- **Get Close:** Your track or track group should fill your frame. Use a macro setting if possible.

- **Include a Scale:** This helps you judge track size.

- **Shoot Straight Down:** Shooting at even a slight angle can distort a track's shape and apparent size.

- **Shoot at Different Exposures:** Many built-in light meters are fooled by sand, snow and mud. Experiment with adjusting the exposure.

- **Take Lots of Pictures:** Take lots of pictures using different settings, then pick out the best to keep.

- **Take Pictures of the Trail and the Surroundings:** Your photographic record will be more useful if you include pictures of the animal's trail and the landscape that it was passing through.

- **Take Notes:** Record where and when you took a picture, as well as information about the surrounding area, for context.

# Track Group Chart

| Track Group | STEP 1: Overall Shape | STEP 2: Number of Toes | STEP 3: Claws Show? | |
|---|---|---|---|---|
| **TINY MAMMALS** | Tracks generally well under 1" | 4 or 5 (front) 5 (hind) | Yes | |
| **SQUIRRELS** | Triangular palm pad, long toes; front foot often shows 2 heel pads | 4 (front) 5 (hind) | Yes | |
| **LARGE RODENTS** | Each track in this group is distinctive | 4 (front) 5 (hind) | Yes | |
| **RABBITS, HARES & PIKA** | Egg-shaped; pads usually indistinct | 4 (front) 4 (hind) | Yes, may be obscure | |
| **SKUNKS** | Compact; stubby toes rarely splay | 5 (front) 5 (hind) | Yes | |
| **WEASELS** | Toes form an arc above chevron-shaped palm pad | 5 (front) 5 (hind) | Yes | |
| **FIVE-TOE WALKERS** | Often resemble human hand prints or footprints | 5 (front) 5 (hind) | Yes | |
| **DOGS** | Oval, large triangular palm pad; claws usually show | 4 (front) 4 (hind) | Yes | |
| **CATS** | Round, very large triangular palm pad; retractable claws rarely show | 4 (front) 4 (hind) | No | |
| **UNGULATES** | Distinctive cloven hoof; prints often heart-shaped | 2 (front) 2 (hind) | Dewclaws | |

*Adventure Quick Guides*

# Only Rocky Mountain Mammal Tracks

## Organized by group for quick and easy identification

## Simple and convenient—narrow your choices by group, and view just a few tracks at a time

- Pocket-sized format—easier than laminated foldouts

- Realistic track illustrations with size information

- Step-by-step guide to track identification

- Track information chart and sample gait patterns

- Based on Jonathan Poppele's popular field guide

Improve your tracking skills with *Animal Tracks* playing cards

**PUBLICATIONS**
**Adventure**
*an imprint of* AdventureKEEN

**NATURE/ROCKY MOUNTAINS**

ISBN 978-1-59193-698-5    **U.S. $9.95**